Other books in this series:
A Knockout of Sports Jokes
A Feast of After Dinner Jokes
A Portfolio of Business Jokes
A Round of Golf Jokes
A Tankful of Motoring Jokes

A Binge of Diet Jokes
A Romp of Naughty Jokes
A Bouquet of Wedding Jokes
A Triumph of Over 50s Jokes
A Megabyte of Computer Jokes

Published simultaneously in 1992 by Helen Exley Giftbooks in the USA, and Helen Exley Giftbooks Ltd in Great Britain.
36 35 34 33 32 31 30
Cartoons © Bill Stott 1992
ISBN 1-85015-351-5
A copy of the CIP data is available from the British Library on request.
Series Editor: Helen Exley
Editor: Elizabeth Cotton
Typeset by Delta, Watford
Printed in China.
Helen Exley Giftbooks Ltd, 16 Chalk Hill, Watford, Herts WD19 4BG, United Kingdom.
Helen Exley Giftbooks LLC, 185 Main Street, Spencer, MA 01562, USA.
www.helenexleygiftbooks.com.

Acknowledgements: The publishers gratefully acknowledge permission to reprint copyright material. They would be pleased to hear from any copyright holders not here acknowledged.
Extracts from *Turning 40* by Dave Barry, reprinted by permission of Random House UK Ltd, Crown Publishing Group, N.Y. and Campbell, Thompson, McLaughlin; extract from *The I Hate To Diet Dictionary* by Sandra Bergeson, reprinted by permission of Turnbull & Willoughby; extracts from *Bald Men Always Come Out On Top* by David E. Beswick, reprinted by permission of Beacon Hill Press of Seattle; extract from *Comic Speeches for Social Occasions*, reprinted by permission of Little, Brown; extract from *The Dieter's Dictionary*, reprinted by permission of Slimming Magazine and Argus Books; extract from *Jokes and Quotes for Speeches* by Peter Eldin, reprinted by permission of Cassell plc; extract from *Jokes For Telling* by Kevin Goldstein-Jackson, reprinted by permission of Elliot Right Way Books; extract from *The Guardian*, reprinted by permission of *The Guardian*; extracts from *You Know You're Forty When* by Herbert Kavet, reprinted by permission of Ivory Tower Publishing Co. Inc.; extract from *The Mother Book* by Liz Smith, reprinted by permission of HarperCollins and Doubleday Inc, N.Y.; extracts from *10,000 Jokes, Toasts and Stories*, reprinted by permission of Doubleday Inc, N.Y.; extracts from *The Public Speaker's Bible* by Stuart Turner, reprinted by permission of HarperCollins; extracts from *Jokes, Quotes and One-Liners* by Herbert V. Prochnow and Herbert V. Prochnow Jr, reprinted by permission of HarperCollins.

A SPREAD OF
OVER 40s'
JOKES

CARTOONS BY
BILL STOTT

EXLEY

So, When Is Old?

"One of the hardest decisions in life is when to start middle age."

HERBERT V. PROCHNOW and HERBERT V. PROCHNOW JR

*

"Old age is always fifteen years older than I am."

BERNARD M. BARUCH

*

"Age is something that doesn't matter, unless you are a cheese."

BILLIE BURKE

*

"Age is a question of mind over matter. If you don't mind, it doesn't matter."

DAN INGMAN

*

"WHY CAN'T YOU BE BORING AND OUT OF TOUCH LIKE
OTHER KIDS' DADS?"

"NO, YOU'RE NOT ADOPTED SO - YES - YOU WILL LOOK LIKE ME

WHEN YOU'RE 42."

THE CHAPTERS OF LIFE

"The four stages of man are infancy, childhood, adolescence and obsolesence."

ART LINKLETTER

*

"**Childhood**: The time of life when you make funny faces in the mirror.
Middle age: The time of life when the mirror gets even."

MICKEY MANSFIELD

*

"The young and old have all the answers. Those in between are stuck with the questions."

HERBERT V. PROCHNOW and HERBERT V. PROCHNOW JR

*

"I was always taught to respect my elders and I've now reached the age when I don't have to respect anybody."

GEORGE BURNS

*

ANCIENT!

"He's so old that when he orders a three-minute egg, they ask for the money up front."

MILTON BERLE

*

"You know you're getting old when you can't go into an antique shop without someone trying to buy you."

P. MACDONALD

*

"He's so old his blood type was discontinued."

BILL DANA

*

"She was so old when she went to school they didn't have history."

RODNEY DANGERFIELD

*

"He's so old he gets winded playing checkers."

ED WYNN

*

"I'LL BE 10 TOMORROW AUNT DOREEN - WERE YOU EVER 10?"

"WHO'S THE CHICK IN THE WHITE DRESS? IT'S ME, YOU RAT!"

The Symptoms

"I don't let old age bother me. There are three signs of old age. Loss of memory... I forget the other two... "

RED SKELTON

*

"Middle-aged spread: unconquered puppy fat."

from *The Dieter's Dictionary*

*

You know you're getting old when everything hurts, and what doesn't hurt, doesn't work.

*

"You know you're getting old when the candles cost more than the cake."

BOB HOPE

*

"Middle age is when your age starts to show around the middle."

BOB HOPE

*

"As we grow older, our bodies get shorter and our anecdotes longer."

ROBERT QUILLEN

*

"You know you've reached middle age when your weightlifting consists merely of standing up."

BOB HOPE

∗

"John Hunt, the Conservative MP for Bromley, Ravensbourne, will ask the Minister today how many deaths can be attributed to jogging during the past five years. Mr Hunt, 49, feels the sport may be 'potentially lethal' for middle-aged people and it would be a good idea to put government health warnings on track suits."

from The Guardian

∗

"YOU'VE GOT A KEEP FIT ATTITUDE PROBLEM."

"I DON'T CARE IF IT HELPS WITH YOUR HOMEWORK OR NOT -
NO I DO NOT REMEMBER THE WAR!"

You know you're over forty when... "You can no longer help the kids with their homework. On the parts you help with, they get 'C-'."

HERBERT I. KAVET, from *You Know You're Over 40 When*

*

"The first half of our lives is ruined by our parents and the second half by our children."

CLARENCE DARROW

"Wrinkles are hereditary. Parents get them from their children."

DORIS DAY

*

Middle age is when you stop criticizing the older generation and start criticizing the younger one.

*

"WHAT DID YOU DO IN THE OLDEN DAYS DAD –
BEFORE T.V. GAMES"

MIDDLE AGE IS . . .

"Middle age is when you are sitting at home on a Saturday night and the telephone rings and you hope it isn't for you."

OGDEN NASH

*

"Middle age is when you're faced with two temptations and you choose the one that will get you home by 9 o'clock."

RONALD REAGAN

*

"Middle age is when you're willing to get up and give your seat to a lady - and can't."

SAMMY KAY

*

"Middle age is that period in life when your idea of getting ahead is staying even."

HERBERT V. PROCHNOW and HERBERT V. PROCHNOW JR

*

"Middle age is when we can do just as much as ever but would rather not."

LAURENCE J. PETER

"DAD'LL BE WITH YOU IN A MINUTE. HE'S JUST PUTTING

HIS TEETH IN."

"YOU FOUND A WRINKLE? GIVE IT 25 YEARS AND YOU WON'T

HAVE TO LOOK FOR THEM...."

MIRROR MIRROR . . .

"If God had to give a woman wrinkles, He might
at least have put them on the soles of her feet."

NINON DE LENCLOS

*

"Time is a great healer, but it's no
beauty specialist."

HERBERT V. PROCHNOW and HERBERT V. PROCHNOW JR

*

"At fifty, everyone has the face he deserves."

GEORGE ORWELL

*

"I have reached the age when I look just as good
standing on my head as I do right side up."

FRANK SULLIVAN

*

"She was 102. She didn't have wrinkles
she had pleats..."

DENNIS WOLFBERG

*

ETERNAL YOUTH

"The only people who really adore being young are the middle aged."

PAM BROWN

*

"MY DAD DOESN'T LOOK 45? WAIT TILL HE STOPS
HOLDING HIS BREATH."

"YEAH, MY DAD'S ON A YOUTH KICK TOO — EVERY TIME WE MEET SOMEONE WHO DOESN'T KNOW ME, HE INTRODUCES ME AS HIS BROTHER...."

"Setting a good example for your children takes all the fun out of middle age."

WILLIAM FEATHER

*

"Youth is a wonderful thing; what a crime to waste it on children."

GEORGE BERNARD SHAW

*

"IT'S FUNNY, ISN'T IT, HOW YOU CAN MAKE YOUR HAIR, SKIN AND FIGURE LOOK YOUNGER - BUT YOU CAN NEVER DANCE YOUNGER?"

PARTYING TO THE END

"It's better to wear out than to rust out."

GEORGE HORNE

"The biggest myth... is that as you grow older, you gradually lose your interest in sex. This myth probably got started because younger people seem to want to have sex with each other at every available opportunity including traffic lights, whereas older people are more likely to reserve their sexual activities for special occasions such as the installation of a new Pope."

DAVE BARRY, from *Turning 40*

*

"This is good news: of memory, hearing, all the faculties - the last to leave us is sexual desire and the ability to make love. That means that long after we're wearing bifocals or hearing aids, we'll be making love. But we won't know with whom."

JACK PAAR

*

"You're still young if the morning after the night before still makes the night before worth the morning after."

BOB GODDARD

"IT'S HER BIRTHDAY AND I SAID SHE DIDN'T LOOK A DAY OVER 50. APPARENTLY, SHE'S 49."

"Age - Something to brag about in your wine-cellar and forget in a birthday book."

from *10,000 Jokes, Toasts and Stories*

*

Birthday Blues

"We were planning to count the candles on his birthday cake... but we were driven back by the heat."

STUART TURNER, from *The Public Speaker's Bible*

*

It was my girl friend's birthday last Wednesday – when I asked her how old she was she said "pushing thirty" but slapped my face when I asked her from which direction.

*

"My wife's best friend has just celebrated the twentieth anniversary of her twenty-ninth birthday."

KEVIN GOLDSTEIN-JACKSON, from *Jokes for Telling*

*

"Don't let years convince you that you are old. Beside a Galapagos tortoise, you are a mere child."

PAM BROWN

*

PITY THE WOMEN!

"Women are most fascinating between the ages of thirty-five and forty, after they have won a few races and know how to pace themselves. Since few women ever pass forty, maximum fascination can continue indefinitely."

CHRISTIAN DIOR

*

"Once upon a time I was so beautiful. My hair was thick and dark and glossy. My skin was smooth and soft as a ripe peach . . . My mouth was dark pink . . . My eyes were large and clear . . . Unfortunately, I was four years old at the time. It's been downhill ever since."

GENEEN ROTH

*

"I have everything now I had twenty years ago - except now it's all lower."

GYPSY ROSE LEE

*

"Inside every slim, beautiful girl, is a fat middle-aged woman waiting to get out."

PAM BROWN

*

"WHEN I WAS 20, GETTING READY TO GO OUT TOOK NO TIME. NOW I'M 40, IT TAKES TWO HOURS. IF I EVER GET TO 80, IT WON'T BE WORTH GOING OUT!"

"Eat, drink and be merry - but remember, it will all catch up with you when you're forty."

PAM BROWN

*

"It's hard to feel fit as a fiddle when you're shaped like a cello."

B.L.

*

You're over the hill when you feel like the morning after and you can swear you haven't been anywhere.

*

"Middle age is when the best exercise is one of discretion."

LAURENCE J. PETER

*

"Except for an occasional heart attack I feel as young as I ever did."

ROBERT BENCHLEY

CONSOLATION FOR BALDNESS

What's the advantage of hair, anyhow?
It blows in your eyes and it flops on your brow,
Disguising the shape of your scholarly head;
It often is gray and it sometimes is red.
Perhaps it is golden and ringleted, but
It needs to be combed and it has to be cut,
And even at best it is nothing to boast of
Because it's what barbarous men have the most of;
Then challenge you mirror, defiant and careless,
For lots of our handsomest people are hairless.

ARTHUR GUITERMAN

*

"God created a few perfect heads; the rest He covered with hair."

DAVID E. BESWICK, from *Bald Men Always Come Out on Top*

✳

"RECEDING HAIR LINE? NONSENSE – I'VE <u>ALWAYS</u> COMBED MY HAIR FORWARD...."

HAIR TODAY . . .

"Middle age is when: Instead of combing your hair, you start 'arranging' it."

HERBERT I. KAVET, from *You Know You're Over 40 When*

✳

"The method preferred by most balding men for making themselves look silly is called the 'comb-over,' which is when the man grows the hair on one side of his head very long and combs it across the bald area, creating an effect that looks... from the top... like an egg in the grasp of a large tropical spider."

DAVE BARRY, from *Turning 40*

✳

"Three Stages of Recession: Hairdo

Hairdid

Hairdone"

DAVID E. BESWICK, from *Bald Men Always Come Out on Top*

✳

THOUGHTS ON FORTY

"Forty is the old age of youth; fifty is the youth of old age."

VICTOR HUGO

"YOU KNOW YOU'RE MIDDLE-AGED WHEN THE DOG LETS YOU GET TO THE STICK FIRST."

"Women over 40 are at their best, but men over 30 are too old to recognize it."

JEAN-PAUL BELMONDO

*

"I am forty now, and forty years is a lifetime; it is extremely old age. To go on living after forty is unseemly, disgusting, immoral! Who goes on living after forty? Give me a sincere and honest answer!"

DOSTOYEVSKY

*

At twenty we don't care what the world thinks of us; at thirty we start to worry about what it thinks of us; at forty we realize that it isn't thinking of us at all.

*

They say life begins at forty - but so do lumbago, bad eyesight, arthritis, and the habit of telling the same story three times to the same person.

*

Is There Sex After Forty?

"You're getting old when you turn out the lights for economic reasons instead of romantic ones."

HERBERT J. KAVET, from *You Know You're Over 40 When . . .*

*

A couple of elderly men were sitting in the park chatting about days gone by, when a pretty young woman came into view and walked past. Seconds later a young man appeared, walking just a bit faster than the young woman, and gaining steadily on her. The first old man gazed after the couple and said, "Do you remember when we used to chase pretty girls down the street?" His friend hardly stirred and replied wearily, "Yes I do remember how we used to chase them, but I can't for the life of me remember why."

"First you forget names, then you forget faces, then you forget to pull your zipper up, then you forget to pull your zipper down."

LEO ROSENBERG

"An old man gives good advice in order
to console himself for no longer being able to set
a bad example."

LA ROCHEFOUCAULD

*

FIT FOR NOTHING

"The only reason I would take up jogging is so I could hear heavy breathing again."

ERMA BOMBECK

"You have to stay in shape. My grandmother, she started walking five miles a day when she was 60. She's 97 today and we don't know where the hell she is."

ELLEN DeGENERIS

"THEY SAY YOU'RE AS YOUNG AS YOU FEEL...
DEPRESSING ISN'T IT?"

At another year
I would not boggle,
Except that when I jog
I joggle.

OGDEN NASH

*

"I'm not into working out. My philosophy: No pain, no pain."

CAROL LEIFER

*

It's Something You Grow Into

"Don't worry about middle age: you'll outgrow it."

LAURENCE J. PETER

*

"Anyone can get old. All you have to do is live long enough."

GROUCHO MARX

*

When in his seventies Sir Malcom Sargent was asked to what he attributed his great age.

"Well," he said, "I suppose I must attribute it to the fact that I haven't died yet."

*

"Old age isn't so bad when you consider the alternative."

MAURICE CHEVALIER

*

"It's not that I'm afraid to die, I just don't want to be there when it happens."

WOODY ALLEN

*

"HE'S 40 TODAY AND LOOKS 50. MIND YOU, WHEN HE WAS 30,

HE LOOKED 40...."

"I CAN'T BELIEVE IT - MY LITTLE BOY 45! YOUR DAD LOOKED
JUST LIKE YOU AT 45. IT'S AMAZING WHAT 20 YEARS WILL DO!"

"Another aid to longevity is that only the good die young."

*

"A local reporter went to interview a man who had just reached the ripe old age of ninety and had entered a marathon.

'Tell me, to what do you attribute your amazing energy and fitness?' he asked.

'Well, I don't drink and I don't smoke and I've never bothered much with women,' the old gent answered.

At this point there was a tremendous crash from upstairs.

'That'll be my father,' the old man said. 'He always gets fresh with the nurse when he's had a few.' "

from *Comic Speeches for Social Occasions*

*

"DANNY AND ME WOULD NEVER PUT YOU IN ONE OF THOSE

PLACES MA - WOULD WE DANNY?"

Old Is . . .

When your son starts treating you with respect.

*

When styles come back for the second time and you still have some left from the first time.

*

When a man says "I want to be alone with you" and you suspect his motives.

*

When you think all of your friends are showing their age . . . but not you.

*

When your husband doesn't embarrass you anymore.

*

When you look in the mirror and think to yourself "Aren't I wise".

MARCELLA MARKHAM, from *Old is Great*

You know you're out of date when:

"You can't name the top ten.

Most of your record collection falls into the 'oldies but goodies' category.

Instead of looking for the action, you look for peace and quiet."

VICTORIA BLACK, from *Moisturizer is my Religion*

*

"You may be certain that age is galloping upon you when, after a feminine voice over the telephone says, 'Do you know who this is?' you say, 'No,' and hang up the receiver."

FRANKLIN P. ADAMS

*

"Life would be infinitely happier if we could only be born at the age of eighty and gradually approach eighteen."

MARK TWAIN

*

"I DON'T WANT TO BE HURTFUL, BUT BUYING RUNNING SHOES LIKE YOUR SON'S JUST MAKES YOU LOOK OLDER!"

"Middle age is when your clothes no longer fit and it's you that needs the alterations."

EARL WILSON

*

"My doctor said I look like a million dollars - green and wrinkled."

RED SKELTON

*

"A middle-aged friend told me that he had been to his doctor for a check-up, after which the doctor said, 'You're in good shape.'

'But, doctor,' he protested, 'why do I keep getting so tired?'

'Youth deficiency,' replied the doctor, 'Nothing but youth deficiency.'"

LEE AIKMAN

*

"Middle age is when you would do anything to feel better except give up what's hurting you."

HERBERT V. PROCHNOW and HERBERT V. PROCHNOW JR

*

"Middle-age is when your medicine chest is better stocked than your drinks cabinet."

PAM BROWN

*

"WE GOT THE TEST RESULTS MR. FITTOCK. INTERNALLY,
YOU'RE AS FIT AS A 20-YEAR-OLD. EXTERNALLY,
YOU JUST <u>LOOK</u> WORN OUT."

"When a man is warned to slow down by a doctor
instead of a policeman."

SIDNEY BRODY

*

"Nothing makes a woman feel older than meeting a bald-headed man who was two grades behind her in school."

HERBERT V. PROCHNOW and HERBERT V. PROCHNOW JR

"DARLING! IT MUST BE 15 YEARS! YOU HAVEN'T CHANGED AT ALL - YOU ALWAYS WERE VERY MATURE...."

*"THAT'S RIGHT, SHE'S BACK DOWN TO THE WEIGHT SHE WAS
WHEN SHE WAS 20. WHAT WE KNOW IS THAT WHEN SHE WAS 20,
SHE WAS 30 POUNDS OVERWEIGHT!"*

"Crash Diet, adj
An invitation to your 10 year class reunion."
SANDRA BERGESON, from *The I Hate to Diet Dictionary*

∗

"Middle age is when your old classmates
are so grey and wrinkled and bald they don't
recognize you."

BENNET CERF

"YOU CAN'T WALK ABOUT LIKE THAT ALL THE TIME. YOU'VE GOT A DOUBLE CHIN - ADMIT IT!"

D<small>ISINTEGRATION</small>

"If I'd known I was going to live so long, I'd have taken better care of myself."

LEON ELDRED

*

"As a person reaching this milestone [your 40th birthday] you need to take time to learn about the biological changes that are taking place within your body, so that you will be better able to understand and cope with the inevitable and completely natural elements of the aging process - the minor aches, pains, dental problems, intestinal malfunctions, muscle deterioration, emotional instability, memory lapses, hearing and vision loss, impotence, seizures, growths, prostate problems, greatly reduced limb function, massive coronary failure, death, and, of course, painful hemorrhoidal swelling - that make up this exciting adventure we call 'middle age'."

DAVE BARRY, from *Turning 40*

*

Falling Apart . . .

"I've got to the age when I need my false teeth and my hearing aid before I can ask where I've left my glasses."

STUART TURNER, from *The Public Speaker's Bible*

*

"You know you're getting old when the gleam in your eye is from the sun hitting your bifocals."

HERBERT V. PROCHNOW and HERBERT V. PROCHNOW JR

*

"Since he started to wear a pace-maker, every time he makes love his garage door opens."

STUART TURNER, from *The Public Speaker's Bible*

*

"You know you're getting older when you try to straighten out the wrinkles in your socks and discover you're not wearing any."

LEONARD L. KNOTT, from *To a Senior with Love*

*

"HAIRPIECE, DENTURES, BIFOCALS - THERE'S NOT A GREAT DEAL OF ME LEFT, IS THERE?"

THE SURGEON'S KNIFE . . .

"This [the facelift] is the procedure wherein the plastic surgeon perks up your face by standing behind you, pulling your skin back on both sides of you head until the front is nice and tight, and then attaching the flaps of excess skin to the back of your head with a staple gun. Sure it stings, but the visual effect is stunning, as you are miraculously transformed from a person with bags and wrinkles into a person whose eyes appear to be just slightly too far apart. In fact, if you get repeated facelifts, your eyes will gradually migrate around to the side of your head, carp-like, and you will experience a real bonus in the peripheral-vision department."

DAVE BARRY, from *Turning 40*

*

"Middle age is when a woman's hair begins to turn from grey to brown."

PETER ELDIN, from *Jokes and Quotes for Speeches*

*

*"HUH! SHE'S HAD SO MUCH LIFTED THAT IF THERE WAS ANY
JUSTICE, SHE'D BE ELEVEN FEET TALL!"*

*

Forty - is the age when you stop patting yourself
on the back and begin under the chin.

*

Twenty-Nine Again?

"I refuse to admit that I'm more than fifty-two,
even if that does make my sons illegitimate."

LADY ASTOR

*

"Mrs. Jacob Adler of the famous Yiddish theatre
family decided to return to acting after a long
interval. A reporter interviewing her asked, 'By the
way, Mrs. Adler, how old are you?'

'I am sixty-one,' she said.

'How odd,' said the reporter. 'I interviewed your
son Jack last week, and he told me he was fifty.'

Mrs. Adler shrugged: 'Oh well, he lives his life
and I live mine.'"

LIZ SMITH, from The Mother Book

*

"As a graduate of the Zsa Zsa Gabor School of
Creative Mathematics, I honestly do not know
how old I am."

ERMA BOMBECK

*

"YOU HAVE TO BE IMPRESSED. HE'S 40 TODAY AND HE CAN
STILL GET INTO HIS FLARES."